Lucy Maud Montgomery

A Writer's Life

written by Elizabeth MacLeod

Kids Can Press

With love to Jennifer, Emily and Sarah Jarvis, all fans of Anne

Acknowledgments

Special thanks to Elizabeth Epperly for reading a draft of this book. Many thanks also to Sally Cohen; Elaine Crawford; Linda Francis and Norma Shephard of the Mobile Millinery Museum; Bev Hayden; Catherine Hunt; Linda Jackson-Hutton and Jack Hutton; Bernard Katz; Ellen Morrison and the staff at the L. M. Montgomery Collection, Archives and Special Collections, University of Guelph; Mary Rubio; and David Wistow.

I'm especially grateful to Patricia Buckley for her patience and tenacity as a photo researcher, designer Karen Powers for her wonderful creativity and much hard work, and Val Wyatt who always edits with good humour, great care and even greater skill. Thanks to everyone who shared with me their stories about Maud and her books. And much love and thanks always to Paul for his support, love, photos and driving!

Excerpts from *My Dear Mr. M.: Letters to G. B. MacMillan from L. M. Montgomery* are reproduced here with the permission of Ruth Macdonald. Published by Oxford University Press, 1992.

Excerpts from *The Alpine Path* by L. M. Montgomery are reproduced here with the permission of David Macdonald, trustee, and Ruth Macdonald. *The Alpine Path: The Story of My Career,* is published by Fitzhenry & Whiteside Ltd., 1975 and 1997.

Quotations from *The Selected Journals of L. M. Montgomery, Volume I* ©1985, University of Guelph, edited by Mary Rubio and Elizabeth Waterston, and published by Oxford University Press, are reproduced with the permission of Mary Rubio, Elizabeth Waterston and the University of Guelph, courtesy of the L. M. Montgomery Collection, Archival and Special Collections, University of Guelph Library.

Other material written by L. M. Montgomery is reproduced here with the permission of David Macdonald, trustee, and Ruth Macdonald.

L. M. Montgomery is a trademark of the Heirs of L. M. Montgomery Inc.

"Anne of Green Gables" and other Images of "Anne" are trademarks and Canadian official marks of the Anne of Green Gables Licensing Authority Inc., located in Charlottetown, Prince Edward Island. All other trademark rights reserved by the Heirs of L. M. Montgomery Inc.

Kids Can Press acknowledges the financial support of the Ontario Arts Council, the Canada Council for the Arts and the Government of Canada, through the BPIDP, for our publishing activity.

Published in Canada by
Kids Can Press Ltd.
29 Birch Avenue
Toronto, ON M4V 1E2

Published in the U.S. by
Kids Can Press Ltd.
2250 Military Road
Tonawanda, NY 14150

Edited by Valerie Wyatt
Designed by Karen Powers
Printed in Hong Kong by Wing King Tong Co. Ltd.

The hardcover edition of this book is smyth sewn casebound.
The paperback edition of this book is limp sewn with a drawn-on cover.

CM 01 0 9 8 7 6 5 4 3 2 1
CM PA 01 0 9 8 7 6 5 4 3 2 1

Canadian Cataloguing in Publication Data

MacLeod, Elizabeth
  Lucy Maud Montgomery : a writer's life

Includes index.
ISBN 1-55074-487-9 (bound)   ISBN 1-55074-489-5 (pbk.)

1. Montgomery, L. M. (Lucy Maud), 1874–1942 — Juvenile literature.
2. Novelists, Canadian (English) — 20th century — Biography — Juvenile
literature.* I. Title.

PS8526.O55Z793 2001   jC813'.52 C00-931683-8
PR9199.3.M6Z79 2001

Kids Can Press is a Nelvana company

Photo credits

Every effort has been made to credit sources of photographs correctly. Please notify the publishers of any discrepancies.

© **Dar Al-Muna**: 29 (middle top right). **Blair W. Anderson Photography**: front cover (bottom left), 5 (top right). **Frank Baldaserra**: 7 (bottom right), 11 (bottom left), 12 (top), 14 (bottom), 23 (top right), back cover (top middle). **Canada Post Corporation**: 3 (top left), 28 (top). **Canadian Film Institute**: 27 (top right), back cover (bottom left). **Collection of Confederation Centre Art Gallery and Museum**, Charlottetown: front cover (background), 11 (middle left), 19 (bottom right), back cover (background). **Courtesy Catherine Hunt**: 8 (bottom left). © **Yumiko Igarashi/Kumon Publishing Co., Ltd. 1997**: 29 (lower top right). © **Klassikerforlaget/illustration © Ben F. Stahl**: 29 (topmost right). **L. M. Montgomery Collection Special Collections University of Guelph** (all photos have been cropped unless specified): front cover (background), 1, 3 (middle left, bottom left [reversed], middle right, bottom right), 4 (top), 5 (middle, bottom right), 6 (top, bottom), 7 (top left, bottom left, top right), 8 (top left [not cropped]), 9 (top left, bottom left, right), 10 (bottom), 11 (top right, lower middle, lower right), 13 (left, middle), 14 (top), 15 (bottom left, top right, bottom right), 16 (bottom), 17 (top left, bottom left background, top right, bottom right), 18 (bottom), 19 (bottom left, top right), 20 (top [not cropped]), 21 (all), 22, 23 (bottom left, middle, bottom right), 24 (top), 25 (all [bottom right not cropped]), 26 (bottom [reversed]), 27 (left, top middle [not cropped], bottom middle), 28 (bottom), 29 (left), back cover (top left, middle left, top right, background). **Parks Canada**: 18 (top), back cover (middle right). **Sharmaine Ryan as Anne Shirley/Photo: Barrett & Mackay**: 29 (lower right). **John Sylvester Photography**: 11 (top left). **Paul R. Wilson Photography**: front cover (top left), 3 (top right), 16 (top).

Cover of Seal Books edition, published by Random House of Canada Limited, reproduced with permission of the publisher (page 4, bottom).

Front and back cover photographs of original edition of *Anne of Green Gables* and L. M. Montgomery are reprinted courtesy of David Macdonald, trustee, and Ruth Macdonald, who are the heirs of L. M. Montgomery and the L. M. Montgomery Collection, Archives and Special Collections, University of Guelph.

Original cover of *Anne of Green Gables* is reprinted courtesy of David Macdonald, trustee, and Ruth Macdonald, who are the heirs of L. M. Montgomery and the L. M. Collection, Archives and Special Collections, University of Guelph Library (page 4, top).

Contents

Meet Lucy Maud Montgomery

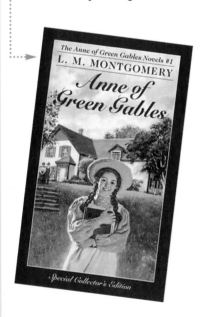

See how different the original edition of *Anne of Green Gables* (above) looks from a modern one? *Anne* was first published almost 100 years ago.

Have you read any of the Anne of Green Gables books? Or the books about Pat of Silver Bush and Emily of New Moon? Ever wondered what the person who wrote them was like?

Lucy Maud Montgomery, who created Anne, Pat and Emily, was one of Canada's first really successful writers. She was a lot like Anne — she gave her favorite places, flowers and trees special names (remember Snow Queen, the beautiful cherry tree outside Anne's window?). And like Pat, Maud loved her home and the beauty of nature. But of all her characters, Maud felt she was most like Emily because they were both writers.

Lucy Maud Montgomery was born on November 30, 1874, in Prince Edward Island. She was named Lucy after one of her grandmothers and Maud after Princess Alice Maud Mary, a daughter of England's Queen Victoria. She hated being called Lucy, preferred Maud and insisted that her name be spelled without an "e."

When Maud was growing up, a woman's life was very different from what it is today. Women couldn't vote or own homes. Most had little schooling. Instead of having careers, women married young and stayed home to raise their children.

But Maud dreamed of another kind of life. She wanted to be an author, even though almost all writers of the time were men. Maud faced many obstacles, but she eventually succeeded. In her lifetime, she wrote 24 books, 530 short stories and more than 500 poems. Her most famous book, *Anne of Green Gables*, has been published in over 20 languages and has sold tens of millions of copies around the world.

Maud's writing has brought happiness to many people. She knew how to tell stories well and had a good sense of humor. She also observed people carefully and seemed to know just which details to use to bring her characters to life.

Where did Maud get ideas for her characters and stories? What was she really like?

Here's the house that I used as the model for Green Gables.

What's a gable? It's the triangular part of a wall that touches the roof.

Maud loved cats. She often included them in her books — and her signature.

"I cannot remember the time when I was not writing, or when I did not mean to be an author. To write has always been my central purpose around which every effort and hope and ambition of my life has grouped itself."

When this picture was taken, Maud was about 43 and at the peak of her writing career.

Early Days

Life in Prince Edward Island was hard when Maud was born. There were no telephones or cars. People traveled in horse-drawn buggies on unpaved roads. Houses were cold in winter — the only heat came from wood-burning stoves and fireplaces.

Before Maud turned two, her mother died of tuberculosis, a lung disease. Soon after, Maud's father moved to Saskatchewan for work. With both parents gone, Maud was brought up by her mother's parents in Cavendish, on the north coast of PEI.

Although her grandparents loved her, they were very strict. Maud had to do as they said and be quiet and ladylike. She was seldom allowed to attend parties or invite friends home.

Maud's grandparents ran the village post office, and in the evenings neighbors would pick up their mail. They'd share stories with Maud's grandfather, stories that Maud remembered all her life. When Maud's friends — who called her Monty or Pollie — came for mail, she had an excuse to go out walking with them.

Maud began school in 1881. She was a good student but sometimes wrote poems when she should have been studying math. She and her friends played tricks on one another and on their teacher. And they had a story club, just like in *Anne of Green Gables*. Their stories had tragic plots and ended with almost everyone dying. Do you remember the story "My Graves" that Anne wrote, then rediscovered in *Anne of the Island*? Maud actually wrote that story when she was about ten years old.

Since no children lived close by, Maud spent a lot of time alone, reading, dreaming — and writing. She wrote about her favorite places, school events, even her cats. Maud also wrote poems. She was especially proud of one called "Evening Dreams" that she wrote when she was about 12 and was anxious to know what others thought of it. Maud worked up her nerve to ask a visiting singer if she'd ever heard a song called "Evening Dreams." When the singer said no, Maud recited her poem. To Maud's relief, the woman liked it. Maud sent her poem to a magazine and a newspaper but neither published it. Other young authors might have given up. But Maud was determined to be a writer.

Maud's grandmother, Lucy Woolner, wasn't unkind to Maud, but she was sometimes cold and formal.

Alexander Marquis Macneill, Maud's grandfather, was stern and irritable. Maud was afraid of him.

Maud never got over the death of her mother, Clara Woolner Macneill. Maud felt that she got her flair for writing from her mother's family.

Here is the house in Clifton (now New London), PEI, where Maud was born. It's about 30 km (19 mi.) northwest of Charlottetown, the provincial capital. You can visit the house — see page 32 for details.

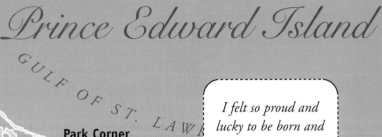

Prince Edward Island

GULF OF ST. LAWR

Park Corner

Bideford
Belmont
Summerside
Bedeque
Cavendish
Clifton

Charlottetown

I felt so proud and lucky to be born and grow up in Prince Edward Island.

Maud was very imaginative and sensitive, which made her feel different and lonely. When she wrote poems, such as "Evening Dreams," she felt better.

Evening Dreams

When the evening sun is setting
Quietly in the west,
In a halo of rainbow glory,
I sit me down to rest.

Growing Up

Hugh John Montgomery was Maud's father. After she left Prince Albert in 1891, Maud never saw him again. He died in 1900.

John Mustard was 22 when he fell in love with 16-year-old Maud. After she refused to marry him, he moved to Toronto to become a minister.

Maud was bursting with excitement! She hadn't seen her father for five years and now she was traveling all the way to Prince Albert, Saskatchewan, to visit him. Maybe she would even live with him and her new stepmother.

In August 1890, at age 15, Maud set off with her paternal grandfather, Senator Donald Montgomery. It took almost two weeks to get to Prince Albert by train. Maud was delighted to see her father, but it soon became clear that she and her stepmother couldn't get along. The stepmother wanted Maud to stay home from school to do housework and look after Maud's stepbrother and stepsister. Maud thought her stepmother was bad tempered, jealous and mean. When Maud finally did get to go to school, she discovered that her classroom was in the same building as the jail!

At school she met Laura and Will Pritchard, and they became best friends. (Years later Maud dedicated *Anne's House of Dreams* to Laura and *Anne of Ingleside* to Will.) Maud didn't think much of her teacher, Mr. Mustard. But he liked her — in fact, he asked Maud to marry him. She coolly refused.

Maud spent her free time with Laura and Will, walking or riding in a horse-drawn carriage. But she always made time for writing. Just before her 16th birthday, Maud wrote the poem "On Cape Leforce," about a duel between two pirates many years before. She mailed the poem to *The Daily Patriot*, a Charlottetown newspaper, then waited for a reply. Weeks went by.

"One afternoon," Maud later recalled, "Father came in with a copy of the *Patriot*. My verses were in it! It was the first sweet bubble on the cup of success and of course it intoxicated me."

Maud's success made her write more. Within a few months, she had poems and an essay published in other newspapers and she won a writing contest run by a Montreal newspaper. She wasn't earning any money, but she was on her way as a writer.

Still, Maud was homesick for PEI. By August 1891, she had had enough of her stepmother. Although Maud was sorry to leave her father and her friends, she returned to the Island.

Sometimes Maud and her friend Laura would sit on the fence around Maud's house and talk.

Here is Maud in 1890, when she headed west to visit her father.

My first poem was published on November 26, 1890, in The Daily Patriot.

Miss Montgomery, Teacher

"I believed in myself and I struggled on alone, in secrecy and silence. I never told my ambitions and efforts and failures to anyone. Down, deep down, under all discouragement and rebuff, I knew I would 'arrive' some day."

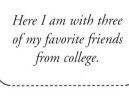

Here I am with three of my favorite friends from college.

At Prince of Wales College, Maud had fun and made many friends.

Brrr! Another morning of getting up early to squeeze in some writing before teaching. Maud's window wouldn't close completely, and she had awoken to find snow on her pillow. But Maud got up and wrote, even though she had to bundle up in her winter coat and tuck her legs under her to keep warm.

When Maud had returned to PEI in 1891, she hoped that her grandfather would pay her college fees so that she could train to be a teacher. But he refused. Instead, Maud moved back into her grandparents' home, where she wrote and taught piano.

Her grandparents found the noise of Maud and her friends too much. They agreed to help her father send Maud back to school. In August 1892, she began preparing for the college entrance exams. She passed them easily, placing fifth out of 264 students.

In the fall of 1893, Maud set off for Prince of Wales College in Charlottetown. There she crammed two years of work into one. She did well on her final exams and in 1894 got a job teaching in Bideford, west of Cavendish.

With her savings from teaching and some money from her grandmother, Maud returned to school in 1895 to study English at Dalhousie University in Halifax, Nova Scotia. She could afford only one year, but she felt it was worth it for her writing.

Maud began teaching again in October 1896. A second cousin, Edwin Simpson, gave Maud his teaching job in Belmont. Ed visited often and soon fell in love with Maud. Maud didn't love him but thought she could learn to, so they became secretly engaged.

In fall 1897, Ed found Maud a job nearby in Lower Bedeque. There, Maud fell madly in love with Herman Leard, a young farmer. Although Maud knew she had so little in common with Herman that they could never marry, she broke up with Ed.

Maud's grandfather died in March 1898, and she returned to Cavendish to live with her grandmother. Maud only saw Herman once more — he died of the flu in June 1899.

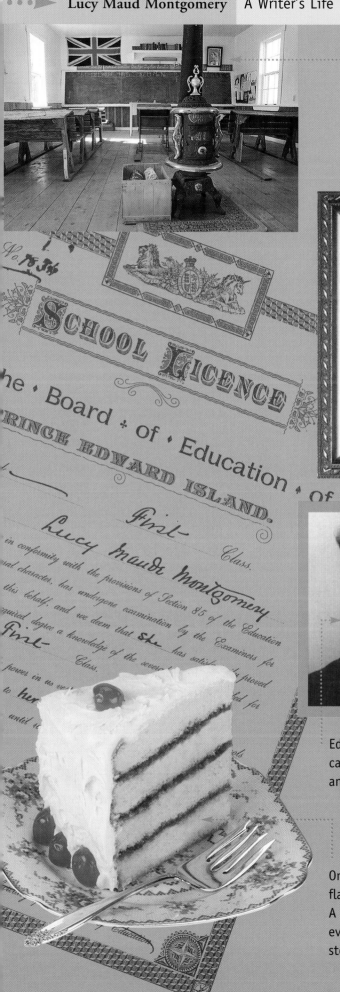

Maud taught in Lower Bedeque from fall 1897 to spring 1898.

Maud's class in Belmont was a mix of grades. She's standing on the far left in this photo.

Edwin Simpson was smart, came from a suitable family and loved Maud deeply.

Maud never had a photo of the man she truly loved, Herman Leard. All she had was this magazine picture of a man who she thought looked just like Herman.

One day Maud's landlady in Bideford accidentally flavored a cake with strong-tasting medicine. A visiting minister ate his piece of cake without even seeming to notice. Later, Maud wove this story into *Anne of Green Gables*.

Newspaper Woman

At Christmas, the *Echo* ran articles about stores that advertised in it. Maud interviewed the shop owners, then wrote the articles. She hated the job — until a hat-store owner promised her a hat if he liked what she wrote. Guess what appeared on Maud's desk a few days later!

I didn't earn much money at the Echo, *but I loved working there and gained a lot of experience.*

Maud spent the next few years writing poems and short stories and looking after her grandmother. Then, in September 1901, she took a job at a newspaper in Halifax. The *Daily Echo* hired her to read the paper before it was printed and make sure it didn't have spelling mistakes or other errors.

One day, the second half of a story disappeared, and Maud was asked to write a new ending. She had never read the missing bit, so she made up a conclusion. Years later, Maud saw the whole story and was amazed at how different the two endings were. She used this experience in *Emily's Quest*.

Maud got a good laugh out of another of her jobs. An assistant editor at the *Echo* started printing a book in the paper, a chapter or so at a time. His boss soon decided that the story was far too long and told Maud to shorten the rest as much as she could. Later, Maud heard a woman talking about the story. The woman described how it had moved so slowly at first, with nothing much happening, then suddenly came to an end. Maud could have explained why! She told a similar story in *Emily Climbs*.

Maud didn't earn much money at the paper. To add to her income, she tried to keep writing articles, stories and poems. But her job left her too tired to write before or after work. So she taught herself to write her stories and poems at the office. She learned to stop in the middle of searching for a rhyme to check an article or answer a visitor's questions. It worked — "L. M. Montgomery" was being published in many top magazines.

The newspaper job ended in June 1902, and Maud knew she had to return to Cavendish to look after her grandmother. She was sorry to leave the *Daily Echo*, but it was time to go back and write in the quiet of her old home.

In her column "Around the Table," Maud signed her name as "Cynthia." One day, Maud wrote about Jonah Days — Anne had one as a teacher in *Anne of Avonlea*.

AROUND THE TABLE

A JONAH DAY

"This has been a Jonah day for me," sighed Kitty, who dropped in the other evening.

"What is a Jonah day," I asked, for the expression was new to me.

"Oh, a day when everything goes wrong," returned Kitty dolefully. "You know when we were children they used to tell us on such a day that we got out on the wrong side of the bed in the morning.

"I felt cross and grumpy when I got up. It poured rain and things were at sixes and all day. I quarreled with Amy and a expected didn't come and I tore a big in my second best skirt, and painted china hairpin plate ush. Oh, you needn't ness or carelessness. It Jonah day and rong."

Maud's office at the *Daily Echo* was on the second floor at the back.

Maud was almost 27 when she began working at the *Echo*. She was the only woman in the office.

Professional Writer

Maud didn't only write stories and poems. She also liked writing letters, especially to her pen pals. She could tell them what she was really thinking, and they understood her in a way that the people around her didn't. Ephraim Weber, who lived in Alberta, was one of her favorite pen pals. They exchanged letters for 40 years.

Maud put down her pen with a sigh. She was tired of writing silly stories. Potboilers she called them, because they earned money to keep the pots boiling on the stove with enough food for her and her grandmother. In 1903, Maud earned $500 from her writing, more than many men earned.

Not all of Maud's stories were published — some were rejected. Maud tried not to be discouraged. Instead, she would quickly send the story to another publisher. Sometimes rejections were good luck for Maud. She once sent a story to a magazine that paid $10. When the story was rejected, Maud sent it to a publisher that paid $30. The story was rejected, but Maud sent it to another magazine. She was finally paid $100 for the story!

Since Maud now ran the post office, she could slip her stories into the mailbag when no one was looking. And she would quickly pull out returned manuscripts before anyone could see them. That way, no one but Maud knew whether a story was accepted or rejected.

Life with Maud's grandmother was tough. The elderly lady told Maud which rooms should be heated and how often she could have a bath (only once a week). Maud was almost 30 and her grandmother still told her when to go to bed.

Maud often felt alone in Cavendish. Most of her friends had married, and many had moved away. Some people thought she was odd because she earned her living as a writer, so they snubbed her. Many men courted her and were hurt when she refused to marry them. Her troubles and worries made her nervous and unhappy. Long walks helped and so did confiding in her diary.

Despite her problems, Maud was determined to keep writing. She soon figured out exactly what kinds of stories the different magazines wanted. She also had the discipline to sit at her desk and write, even when she didn't feel like it. Maud wrote and sent out lots of stories. She also began to wonder if she could write a book ...

"By 1901 I was beginning to make a 'livable' income for myself by my pen, though that did not mean everything I wrote was accepted on its first journey. Far from it. Nine out of ten manuscripts came back to me. But I sent them out over and over again, and eventually they found resting places."

I loved dressing up with hats and parasols and having my picture taken.

Taking photos was one of Maud's favorite hobbies. She was a good photographer and experimented with special effects, but many of her photos are on a slight tilt, like the one below. Maud even created her own darkroom, where she developed her pictures.

Here is Maud at about age 28.

Maud made this crazy patchwork cushion cover in 1901. She was a good sewer and combined her colors and patterns with flair.

Writing *Anne of Green Gables*

Where did Anne Shirley's last name come from? Not long before Maud began writing *Anne of Green Gables*, a friend brought her some field poppies, also known as Shirley poppies. The name may have stuck with Maud.

Maud saw this photo in a magazine and decided this was how Anne looked. Maud never knew that it was a photo of Evelyn Nesbit, a New York showgirl from the early 1900s.

In the spring of 1905, Maud was looking through an old notebook filled with notes for characters, descriptions and plots. She was searching for an idea for a short story when something she had written caught her eye: "Elderly couple apply to orphan asylum for a boy. By mistake a girl is sent them."

Right away Maud began to think about what that girl might be like and what might happen to her. The girl's name even flashed into Maud's mind — Anne-with-an-E. Maud hated when people spelled her name "Maude," so she knew how important it would be to Anne to have her name spelled correctly.

And Anne had to have red hair. When Maud was studying for the college entrance exams, she'd had fun teasing a boy in her class about his red hair. Maud pictured Anne as lively and, well, gingery, and so she needed ginger-colored hair.

Because Maud never felt she belonged in her grandparents' home, she was determined to give Anne a good home. Maud had always liked a neighbor's house with its green gables, and she adopted it as Anne's home. Maud called it "Green Gables."

As Maud plotted out the short story, Anne seemed to come alive. The more Maud worked on Anne, the more she liked her. Was this the idea for a book that she had been waiting for?

One rainy night in May 1905, Maud began writing Anne's story. She wrote a few paragraphs, then put down her pen and reread them. As she picked up her pen to continue, Ewen Macdonald, a local minister, walked in. They chatted all evening, so Maud got no more writing done that night.

But Maud was soon at work on *Anne* again. Between writing stories to pay bills and looking after her grandmother and the post office, Maud had little time. So while washing dishes or gardening, she worked out dialogue. As she hung laundry or swept floors, she thought about plot.

Maud wrote her story by hand, in the kitchen or her bedroom. She was determined to tell Anne's story to the best of her abilities. Maud knew that if she did, it could mean a new life for her.

This is the kitchen where Maud wrote about Anne. She sat on the kitchen table, close to the window, where she could get the last of the day's light.

Ewen Macdonald was the minister who interrupted Maud one evening when she had just begun writing about Anne.

"I was beginning to think of writing a book. It had always been my hope and ambition to write one. But I never seemed able to make a beginning. Besides, I did not see just how I could get time for it. I could not afford to take the time from my regular writing hours."

Like Anne, Maud called one of her favorite paths "Lover's Lane."

Whenever I felt tired or lonely, I'd go walking in Lover's Lane. It always lifted my spirits.

Maud was in her early 30s when she wrote Anne's story.

Rejection

a n n e
of
g r e e n

Maud could afford only a secondhand typewriter. It didn't type capital letters very well and wouldn't print the letter "w" at all.

One of Maud's favorite places was this forest near her home. She named it the Haunted Wood and included it in *Anne of Green Gables*. And, like Anne, Maud began to believe the ghost stories she created about it and became terrified by the wood.

It took Maud months to finish telling Anne's story. Finally, in October 1905, she was ready to have it published. Maud typed out the manuscript, carefully chose a publisher, then proudly and hopefully sent off *Anne of Green Gables*. And the publisher sent it right back.

Maud wasn't discouraged — her stories had been rejected many times. She simply mailed the manuscript to another publisher. And that publisher sent it back! Maud sent Anne's story to five publishers — and all of them rejected it. For the first time, Maud was truly disheartened. Perhaps she should be content writing her potboilers and poems. After all, they paid the bills.

Brushing away a tear, Maud tucked *Anne* into an old hatbox and put the box in a cupboard. Later, when it didn't hurt so much, she planned to see if she could turn it into a short story.

Maud forgot about Anne and her dream of writing a book. She was busy writing her potboilers, poems and even a hymn about PEI. But months later, as she was sorting through the cupboard, Maud pulled out the manuscript and read it again. As she turned the pages, she became more and more excited. Her story didn't seem so bad. Why not try again? Maud packaged up *Anne* and once more sent out her story, this time to the American publisher L. C. Page & Company.

At last Maud's book was accepted! As she stood with the publisher's acceptance letter in her hands, she could hardly believe her eyes. The dream she had cherished for so long had finally come true.

On June 20, 1908, a very special package arrived in the mail for Maud. Trembling, she undid the wrapping. There was her book, *Anne of Green Gables*. "My first book," wrote Maud in her diary. "Not a great book, but mine, mine, mine ..."

"Well, I've written my book! The dream dreamed years ago at that old brown desk in school has come true at last after years of toil and struggle."

Patriotic Hymn of Prince Edward Island
———◆———

Fair Island of the sea
We raise our song to thee,
The bright and blest:
Loyally now we stand
As brothers hand in hand,
And sing God save the land
We love the best.

*— words by L. M. Montgomery,
1908*

As you can see, I changed my mind and corrected as I wrote.

This was Maud's bedroom for more than 30 years. She loved the room, where she could be alone to think or dream or write.

When Maud pulled *Anne* out of the hatbox, months after she'd sadly put it away, she intended to rework it into a short story. She thought she could earn $35 to $40 for it. Little did she know what it would one day earn her.

Life after Anne

FICTION

L. M. MONTGOMERY — a face of balance and refinement. The smooth high forehead shows love of stories and sympathetic perception, the height and squareness above the temples and arched eyebrows suggest poetic feeling and artistic taste, while the full eyes show facility of expression.

I liked this magazine description of me so much that I pasted it into my journal.

"Anne is as real to me as if I had given her birth," Maud wrote in her diary, "as real and as dear." She hoped that *Anne of Green Gables* would be a success, but she never dreamed that so many people would love it. *Anne* was a best-seller right away.

Soon Maud became famous worldwide and, to her amazement, not only with children. Canada's governor general and Great Britain's prime minister were fans. Mark Twain, who wrote about Tom Sawyer and Huckleberry Finn, even sent her a fan letter.

Maud's publisher offered her $500 or a small payment (called a royalty) for each book sold. Which would you choose? Luckily, Maud chose the royalty. Her first payment alone was $1730. At the time, that would have bought several houses in PEI.

Before *Anne of Green Gables* was published, Maud's publisher insisted that she write a second book about Anne. She loved telling Anne's story again but found the writing difficult because she hadn't planned to create a series. Maud also had to write *Anne of Avonlea* quickly to satisfy her publisher.

Sometimes Maud took breaks from writing. She was proud to be invited to a party to meet Earl Grey, Canada's governor general. He asked her to go for a walk so they could chat about her books. They strolled along, then Earl Grey suggested that they sit on the steps of a nearby building. He didn't realize the building was an outhouse! Maud could hardly keep from laughing.

Anne of Green Gables was becoming more popular. It was translated into Swedish and Dutch, which earned Maud more money. In 1910, Maud received royalty payments totaling $7000. The average worker in PEI earned less than $300 a year.

With all this money, you'd think that Maud's life would become easier. But her grandmother wouldn't let her make any changes to their house to make it more comfortable. And Maud couldn't leave her grandmother by herself, so she couldn't travel.

One part of Maud's life *was* easier. After *Anne* was published, she got requests for stories from magazines that had once turned her down. Now it seemed they would take anything she wrote.

WHETHER Miss L. M. Montgomery is a Canadian or not, we know not, but if she isn't she has taken a Canadian countryside, and peopled it, in a manner marvellously natural, and if she is a Canadian she has succeeded in writing one of the few Canadian stories that can appeal to the whole English-speaking world. "Anne of Green Gables," is a charmingly-told story of life on the north shore of Prince Edward Island, but the local coloring is most delicately placed on the canvas and in no respect we the impression created by the figure, Anne. This waif of orphan asylum in Nov adopted by an old farm maiden sister, is cove sensitive and imaginati the story of her hopes ambitions, will appea old and young. She the most attractive fiction has yet racters of the with reached

Anne of Green Gables received some bad reviews but most were glowing. Maud loved reading the good reviews.

When Maud received her invitation to meet the governor general, she had nothing suitable to wear. This dress was made for her in less than five days.

A HEROINE FROM AN ASYLUM

A farmer in Prince Edward's Island ordered a boy from a Nova Scotia asylum, but the order got twisted and the result was that a girl was sent the farmer instead of a boy. That girl is the heroine of L. M. Montgomery's story, "Anne of the Green Gables," (L. C. Page & Co.) and it is no exaggeration to say that she is one of the most extraordinary girls that ever came out of an ink pot. The author undoubtedly meant her to be queer, but she is altogether too queer. She was only 11 years old when she reached the house in Prince Edward's Island that was to be her home, but, in spite of

Cavendish. P.E.I. Saturday. June 20. 1908 To-day has been, or *Anne herself* would say "an epoch in my life." My book came to-day, fresh from the publishers. I candidly confess that it was for me a proud, wonderful, thrilling moment! There in my hand lay the material realization of all the dreams and hopes and ambitions and struggles...

This is what Maud wrote in her journal when she received her first copy of *Anne of Green Gables*.

Mrs. Macdonald

Because of the money she earned from *Anne of Green Gables,* Maud could afford to buy lots of beautiful clothes for her honeymoon.

Maud had a secret. She'd kept it for almost five years and only one other person knew it — Ewen Macdonald. He was the Presbyterian minister who had interrupted her the night she began writing about Anne. What was their secret? On October 12, 1906, Maud had become engaged to marry Ewen.

Ewen Macdonald was born in Prince Edward Island of Scottish ancestors, just like Maud. These things were important to her. Maud admired Ewen's education and thought him quite handsome, while Ewen had been interested in Maud from the first time he saw her. But Maud couldn't leave her grandmother to marry Ewen. They would have to wait until Maud's grandmother died before they could marry.

Soon after Maud and Ewen became engaged, he left to study for a year in Scotland. When he came back, he was the minister at two churches some distance from Cavendish. Then, in March 1910, Ewen became the minister of churches in Leaskdale and Zephyr, Ontario. Although Maud and Ewen were engaged, they didn't spend much time together and had little chance to really get to know each other.

Maud's grandmother died of pneumonia on March 5, 1911. Maud was heartbroken. While her grandmother had been difficult, she had helped put Maud through school and had given her a home. Maud thought of her as a mother.

But now Maud was free to marry Ewen. Their wedding was held on July 5, 1911, and soon after, they left for a long honeymoon in England and Scotland. Maud was delighted to be going to the land of her ancestors. And she also looked forward to meeting George Boyd MacMillan, a pen pal she'd been writing to for almost ten years.

When Maud and Ewen's honeymoon was over, they returned to Canada, to Ewen's home in Leaskdale. Maud was so happy to live in a house of her own, even though her new home was far away from the Island she loved. For the rest of her life, she lived in Ontario.

"Somehow then, I felt that I could not let [Ewen Macdonald] go out of my life. He seemed to belong in it. I couldn't face the thought of the emptiness and blankness he would leave."

Ewen and I were married at noon, and my cousin Frede prepared a delicious dinner after the ceremony.

Mr. and Mrs. John Ca[...] announce the marriage of their niece Lucy Maud Montgomery to Rev. Ewen Macdonald, B.A. on Wednesday the fifth of July nineteen hundred and eleven at Park Corner, P.E.I.

Maud and Ewen loved visiting Scotland on their honeymoon. Here they are in Glasgow.

In Scotland, Maud finally met one of her favorite pen pals, George Boyd MacMillan, who was also a writer. Maud dedicated *Emily of New Moon* to him.

Life in Leaskdale

"Frede," as Maud called her cousin Fredericka Campbell, was Maud's best friend.

I gave Frede the money to go to college. She was such a good friend and I was delighted to be able to help her.

A year after Maud was married, she gave birth to a son, Chester. A second son was stillborn about two years later, which devastated Maud. The safe birth of Stuart in 1915 was a great relief to her.

Maud now wrote every morning, then spent the rest of the day with her sons or doing church work. She trained Chester and Stuart not to interrupt her when she worked, but sometimes they pushed flowers under her door to get her attention.

By 1914, Maud's income reached $12 000 — as much as Canada's prime minister made. Later, it soared to $46 000. When Maud published *Rilla of Ingleside*, she vowed it would be the last book in the Anne series. (Actually, she wrote two more.) Maud had a new character she wanted to write about — Emily of New Moon. It took Maud only six months to complete the first Emily book, the shortest time of any of her novels.

In 1916, Maud's contract with publishers L. C. Page & Company ended, and she switched to the Canadian publisher McClelland, Goodchild and Stewart. Page didn't want to lose such a valuable author and found reasons to take Maud to court. The company also published *Further Chronicles of Avonlea* without Maud's permission, so she sued. The lawsuits dragged on for years.

Adding to Maud's troubles was her horror at World War I. The thought of all the young men dying in battle caused her great despair. But Maud had bigger problems. Her cousin and dearest friend, Fredericka Campbell, died of pneumonia in January 1919. Frede's death was a terrible blow to Maud.

A few months later, Ewen began to suffer from headaches, sleeplessness and depression. Maud was afraid to tell anyone because she thought Ewen would lose his job. When he was too sick to preach, she said he had a headache. Although Ewen was hospitalized many times, Maud covered up so well that even their maids had no idea he was very ill.

But not everything was bleak in Maud's life. In January 1923, she became the first Canadian woman to be named a Fellow of the Royal Society of Arts in England. A few months later, she won a large lawsuit against her publisher. With that behind her, Maud could once again concentrate on her writing.

"Leaskdale is a very pretty country place ... only forty miles from Toronto. I find the people here nice and kind ... We have a nice brick manse, prettily situated, though too close to the other houses and backyards in the village to suit my love of solitude and retirement."

Maud thought this photo, taken in 1924, looked more like her than any other.

Do you remember the china dogs Gog and Magog that Anne fell in love with in *Anne of the Island*? They looked like these dogs, which Maud bought on her honeymoon. Like one of Anne's sons, Maud's son Chester once introduced them to a visitor as "God and My God."

This photo of Maud's husband and sons was taken in 1917, when Stuart (left) was almost two and Chester was five.

This girl looks just the way Maud pictured Emily of New Moon. Maud also noticed that the artist included an old moon, not a new one!

Emily, Pat and Marigold

In 1925, some people in Ewen's churches voted to join the United Church, a church made up of Presbyterians and Methodists. Ewen was against this union and left Leaskdale in 1926 to become the minister at the Presbyterian churches in Norval and Union, Ontario, about 80 km (50 mi.) away. Maud was sad to leave Leaskdale, but the manse (minister's home) in Norval was beautiful, and it was her first home with electricity.

The people of Norval were proud that their minister's wife was a famous author. They got used to seeing her talking to herself as she ran errands — Maud still worked out dialogue and plots in her spare moments. Her neighbors were especially proud in 1927, when Maud met the Prince of Wales and Prince George of England. Even Great Britain's prime minister asked to meet her.

Maud grew to love Norval. She made some close friends there and was pleased with her house. She also began working on a new heroine, Marigold. In *Magic for Marigold*, Marigold's home was called "Cloud o' Spruce" because of the spruce forest on the hill behind it. Those woods were based on the hill of pines Maud could see from her bedroom in Norval.

Lucky was one of Maud's favorite cats. She dedicated her book *Jane of Lantern Hill* to him.

Maud won her last lawsuit against her publisher, L. C. Page & Company, in 1928. But the next year, she lost a lot of money when the stock market crashed. She could no longer give friends and relatives money as she once did. She wanted to write less but found herself working harder than ever. To add to her troubles, she had to have all her teeth pulled because they were causing so much pain.

And Ewen's health was failing. By the early 1930s, he'd spend days in bed, moaning or singing. Maud struggled to keep his illness a secret, but she feared that people would soon find out.

Despite the hard times, Maud accomplished a lot during her nine years in Norval. She published six books, including *Emily's Quest* and both books about Pat of Silver Bush, one of her few characters who had two parents. Maud also published her only books for adults, *The Blue Castle* and *A Tangled Web*, while living in Norval.

Maud thought the leading actress in the 1934 movie of *Anne of Green Gables* looked just right. The actress even used the stage name "Anne Shirley," which was Anne's full name.

Maud was delighted to meet the Prince of Wales and bought a new hat for the occasion.

In the honour of meeting H.R.H. The Prince of Wales

His Honour The Lieutenant Governor and Mrs. William D. Ross request the company of Rev. Ewan Macdonald; Mrs L. M. Macdonald at a Garden Party on Saturday, the 6th of August, 1927

An answer is requested to the Secretary

I loved directing plays. Here's one of the theater groups I worked with.

"*My new book* Pat of Silver Bush *came out in September ... I really put more of myself into Pat than into any other of my heroines.*"

Final Words

Stamps have been issued in honor of Lucy Maud Montgomery. Ferries, trains and university buildings — even golf course holes — have been named after her.

King George V presented Maud this Officer in the Order of the British Empire medal in September 1935.

In March 1935, Ewen retired and Maud bought them a house in Toronto, on the Humber River. It was the first house Maud had ever owned — the manses she lived in had belonged to the churches. She called the house "Journey's End" because she hoped she would never have to move out of it. She never did.

By now, L. M. Montgomery was famous in Europe, as well as in Canada. Maud was elected to the Literary and Artistic Institute of France, one of France's highest honors. Very few women or people from outside France are made members of this academy. Six months later, Maud was also made an Officer in the Order of the British Empire.

The last few years of Maud's life were very hard. Ewen became more and more ill. World War II started in 1939, and Maud was terrified that her sons would be killed in it. After coping with so many worries for so many years, her health began to seriously break down in 1941.

Maud died on April 24, 1942, and is buried in Cavendish, where she grew up. She never knew how incredibly popular her characters would become around the world. Movies, musicals, plays and television shows have introduced many people to Anne and Emily. A musical version of *The Blue Castle* is one of the favorite musicals of Poland.

In Japan, *Anne of Green Gables* is widely known and loved. A Canadian missionary left a copy of the book with a Japanese woman when the missionary fled Japan before World War II. The woman translated the book into Japanese. It was one of the first English-language books available in Japanese and, for many years, one of the few books for Japanese teenagers. Japanese people appreciate Anne's love of nature, her imagination, spirit and discipline. Today, Japan has clubs and theme parks dedicated to Anne.

Despite problems that would have discouraged most people, Maud was determined to be a writer, and she succeeded beyond her wildest dreams. She has delighted millions of readers all over the world for many years. Thanks to the wonderful characters Maud created, she will never be forgotten.

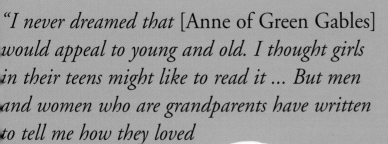

"I never dreamed that [Anne of Green Gables] would appeal to young and old. I thought girls in their teens might like to read it ... But men and women who are grandparents have written to tell me how they loved Anne, and boys at college have done the same."

Anne of Green Gables has been translated into many languages, including (from top) Swedish, Arabic and Japanese.

Maud was in her 60s when she moved to Journey's End.

For more than 35 years, the musical *Anne of Green Gables* has been performed every summer in Charlottetown.

Maud's Life at a Glance

1874 November 30 — Lucy Maud Montgomery is born in Clifton (now New London), Prince Edward Island

1876 Maud's mother dies. Maud's father moves west to Saskatchewan and leaves Maud with her mother's parents

1881 Maud starts school in Cavendish, PEI

1890 August 16 — Maud arrives in Prince Albert, Saskatchewan, to visit her father and stepmother

November 26 — Maud is published for the first time. Her poem "On Cape Leforce" is published in *The Daily Patriot*

1891 August 25 — Maud leaves Prince Albert to return to PEI

1893 September — Maud begins a teachers training course at Prince of Wales College in Charlottetown, PEI

1894 July — Maud teaches for the first time at Bideford, PEI

1895 September — Maud begins studying English at Dalhousie University in Halifax, Nova Scotia

1896 February — Maud earns money from her writing for the first time. She begins teaching in Belmont, PEI

1897 June 8 — Maud is secretly engaged to Edwin Simpson, her second cousin

1897 Maud teaches for a year in Lower Bedeque, PEI. She falls in love with Herman Leard, a young farmer

1898 March — Maud breaks her engagement with Edwin Simpson

March 5 — Maud's grandfather dies. Maud returns to Cavendish to live with her grandmother

1899 June 30 — Herman Leard dies

1900 January 16 — Maud's father dies

1901–1902 Maud works at the *Daily Echo*, a Halifax newspaper

1905 May — Maud begins writing *Anne of Green Gables*

1906 October 12 — Maud becomes engaged to Reverend Ewen Macdonald

1908 June — *Anne of Green Gables* is published

1911 March 5 — Maud's grandmother dies

July 5 — Maud marries Ewen Macdonald. They move to Leaskdale, Ontario

1912 July 7 — Maud's first child, Chester Cameron, is born

1914 August 13 — Maud's second son, Hugh Alexander, is stillborn

1915 October 7 — Maud's third son, Ewan Stuart, is born

1916	Maud leaves her publisher, L. C. Page & Company, to move to McClelland, Goodchild and Stewart (now known as McClelland & Stewart)
1919	January 25 — Fredericka Campbell, Maud's cousin and best friend, dies
1923	January — Maud becomes the first Canadian woman to become a Fellow of the Royal Society of Arts in England
1926	February — Ewen becomes the minister at the Presbyterian churches in Norval and Union, Ontario. Maud and family move into the manse in Norval
1927	August — Maud meets the Prince of Wales and Prince George in Toronto
1928	Maud wins her last lawsuit against L. C. Page & Company
1935	March — Ewen retires from the ministry. The family moves to Toronto
	March 9 — Maud is elected to the Literary and Artistic Institute of France
	September — Maud is made an Officer in the Order of the British Empire
1942	April 24 — Maud dies. She is buried in Cavendish, PEI

Maud's Books

How many of Lucy Maud Montgomery's books have you read? Did you know that Maud didn't write the Anne books in the order of Anne's life? The number after each one tells you the order in which to read them.

Published	Title
1908	Anne of Green Gables (1)
1909	Anne of Avonlea (2)
1910	Kilmeny of the Orchard
1911	The Story Girl (*this was Maud's favorite*)
1912	Chronicles of Avonlea
1913	The Golden Road
1915	Anne of the Island (3)
1916	The Watchman and Other Poems
1917	Anne's House of Dreams (5)
	The Alpine Path
1919	Rainbow Valley (7)
1920	Further Chronicles of Avonlea
1920	Rilla of Ingleside (8)
1923	Emily of New Moon
1925	Emily Climbs
1926	The Blue Castle
1927	Emily's Quest
1929	Magic for Marigold
1931	A Tangled Web
1933	Pat of Silver Bush
1935	Mistress Pat
1936	Anne of Windy Poplars (4)
1937	Jane of Lantern Hill
1939	Anne of Ingleside (6)

Which one is your favorite?

These books were published after Maud died:

1974	The Road to Yesterday
1979	The Doctor's Sweetheart
1985, 1987, 1992, 1998	The Selected Journals of L. M. Montgomery, vols. 1, 2, 3, 4
1987	The Poetry of L. M. Montgomery
1988	Akin to Anne
1989	Along the Shore
1990	Among the Shadows
1991	After Many Days
1993	Against the Odds
1994	At the Altar
1995	Across the Miles
1995	Christmas with Anne

Visit Maud

In Prince Edward Island:

Green Gables House in Cavendish is the house on which Maud based her idea of Anne's home. You can see Maud's old typewriter there. At the **Anne of Green Gables Museum** at Silver Bush, Park Corner, see where Maud was married, family photos and more. **The Lucy Maud Montgomery Birthplace** displays Maud's wedding dress and scrapbooks.

In Ontario:

At **Leaskdale** and **Norval** you can see the manses where Maud lived and the churches where Ewen preached. **Bala's Museum with Memories of Lucy Maud Montgomery** is in the building where Maud and her family ate during a holiday in Muskoka.

Web Sites

There are many Web sites about Maud and her books. Here are a few:

www.geocities.com/Athens/Parthenon/2544/letter.html

club.pep.ne.jp/~r.miki/index_e.htm

www.upei.ca/~lmmi/

www.bala.net/museum/

These two Web rings will lead you to other sites:

www.webring.org/cgi-bin/webring?ring=anne;list

www.webring.org/cgi-bin/webring?ring=kindredspirits&list

Index